Michael Lawson Brown

The Empty Water Tank

Illustrated by
Tony Morris

Series Editor: Karen Morrison

Heinemann Educational Publishers
A division of Heinemann Publishers (Oxford) Ltd
Halley Court, Jordan Hill, Oxford OX2 8EJ

Heinemann Educational Books (Nigeria) Ltd
PMB 5205, Ibadan
Heinemann Educational Boleswa
PO Box 10103, Village Post Office, Gaborone, Botswana

FLORENCE PRAGUE PARIS MADRID
ATHENS MELBOURNE JOHANNESBURG
AUCKLAND SINGAPORE TOKYO
CHICAGO SAO PAULO

© Michael Lawson Brown 1996
First published by Heinemann Educational Publishers in 1996
The right of Michael Lawson Brown to be identified as the author of this work has been
asserted by him in accordance with the Copyright, Designs and Patents Act 1988

British Library Cataloguing in Publication Data
A catalogue record for this book is available
from the British Library

ISBN 0 435 89178 2

Glossary

Difficult words are listed alphabetically on page 29

Edited by Christine King
Designed by The Point
Printed and bound in Great Britain

96 97 98 99 10 9 8 7 6 5 4 3 2 1

Most people can remember a time of terrible drought in southern Africa.

On the farms, the land is bone dry, and the earth is dusty. The crops fail. The cattle become stick thin.

In the towns, the taps are dry. People try hard to save water. They pour dirty washing water on to the plants in their gardens.

Droughts can cause death and hardship. Each year, people hope that there will be no drought.

One year in Mutare, the drought was very bad. The town had no rain at all during the year. Not a drop!

The rivers and streams all dried up. The storage dams outside the town became smaller and smaller.

Each family was allowed one hundred litres of water each day. But as the drought continued, there was a new law in the town. For three days of the week, all the taps were turned off. There was no water at all then.

Everyone in Mutare suffered. Rich people and poor people had their taps turned off. Mr Munemo was one of the richest men in the town, but his taps were also dry.

Mr Munemo was not pleased about this. He watched his garden slowly die. He became very angry.

'Why can't I have any water?' he grumbled. 'I have plenty of money. I can pay for extra water.'

Mr Munemo made a plan. First, he built a tall iron platform in his garden. Then he bought a huge metal tank and placed it on the platform. This cost a lot of money.

'That's ugly,' said a neighbour, pointing at the tank. 'What is it for?'

'Water,' explained Mr Munemo.

'Phew,' said the neighbour, 'that tank can hold enough water for a month, but why? There is no water in Mutare.'

'I know,' said Mr Munemo. He smiled and went into his house.

Mr Munemo knew a farmer who lived across the mountains. This farmer had a deep borehole on his land. He pumped up water every day from under the ground to water his crops.

Mr Munemo drove there in his big car and said to the farmer, 'Can I have some of your water?'

'You must pay for it,' said the farmer, 'and carry it yourself.'

'I have plenty of money,' said Mr Munemo. 'I'll hire a truck.'

And he did.

At home, Mr Munemo boasted to his neighbour. He liked to tell people what he could buy with his money.

He said, 'Tomorrow I'll have enough water for my family to have a bath every day. I can use the water on my flowers and vegetables. The fruit will grow fat and sweet on the trees. My grass will be green too.'

'You're a lucky man, Mr Munemo,' said the neighbour sadly.

The next morning, a large truck arrived at Mr Munemo's house. It was pulling a big green water container on wheels.

The driver slowly steered his truck through the gate. There was not much space. He needed to get close to the water tank, so he drove on to the grass.

'Watch my lawn!' shouted Mr Munemo. 'Don't destroy my flowers!'

The driver climbed out of his truck. He pulled a hose out from the water container on his truck, and put the end into the tank. Then he started the pump motor and water began to flow into Mr Munemo's tank.

'Very good!' said Mr Munemo. 'Very good indeed!' He was very happy.

Many neighbours had heard the sound of the pump. They came to see what was happening.

'Mr Munemo is a lucky man,' they said. 'He will have enough water now.'

At last the water tank was full. The driver turned his truck around once more on the lawn.

'Be careful of the flowers!' Mr Munemo shouted again. But it was too late! His beautiful flowers were crushed beneath the huge wheels.

The driver just waved. He drove carefully through the iron gate posts and turned into the road.

'Aiyee!' shouted the neighbours. They knew what was going to happen.

The driver had forgotten the water container behind his truck. There was a loud noise as it bumped into the gate. The gate was torn from its post.

Mr Munemo ran down the driveway.

'Look what you've done!' he shouted angrily. 'Look at my gate!'

The driver was also angry.

'Look at my water container!' he shouted. 'It has a hole in it. Now I'll have to fix it.'

He drove his truck away in a rage.

Mr Munemo looked at his broken gate. The neighbours looked too and shook their heads. The iron was twisted and broken.

'What will you do now, Mr Munemo?' asked one of the neighbours.

Mr Munemo glared at him. 'I'll have it fixed of course,' he snapped. 'Today!'

He marched up his driveway and into his house. He went straight to his telephone. Mr Munemo always did what he said he would do. He was a proud man.

Later that morning, a van came to Mr Munemo's house. A man climbed out. He was wearing overalls with 'Mutare Welders' printed on the back.

The welder looked carefully at the gate, and then he said to Mr Munemo, 'I can fix your gate, but it will cost a lot of money.'

Mr Munemo sighed. 'Of course it will,' he said. 'Carry on. Just fix it as quickly as you can.'

The man went back to his van and took out his tools. He began to hammer the twisted gate back into shape. He was a strong man and he worked hard.

Mr Munemo smiled happily and returned to his house.

Then the man got his welding torch and a gas bottle from his van. He fitted the torch to the gas bottle. He pressed a button. A fierce blue flame leapt out of the welding torch.

The welder put on a pair of dark glasses to protect his eyes. The flame from the welding torch softened the iron gate. Bright sparks splashed in all directions. Slowly, he welded the broken pieces of iron together.

A tall hedge grew next to the gate along the front of Mr Munemo's garden. Because of the drought, this hedge was very dry.

The sparks from the welding torch jumped on to the hedge and also on to the dead grass. But no one noticed. A small flame quickly grew and soon the bottom of the hedge was alight. By the time a neighbour saw the flame, it was too late. The whole hedge was burning.

The fire raced along the hedge. It crackled and spat, making more sparks than the welding torch. Soon the whole hedge was alight with blue, yellow and orange flames.

'Aiyee!' shouted the people. 'Watch out!' they called to the welder. 'You'll be burnt.'

The man looked up from his work. He was lucky. The wind had blown the fire away from him. He switched off his torch and moved away quickly, carrying the gas bottle.

Mr Munemo was not so lucky. The wind sent the sparks from the hedge towards his house. The dry lawn burnt quickly.

'My house will catch fire!' screamed Mr Munemo.

'Call the Fire Brigade!' shouted the welder. 'Hurry!'

Mr Munemo ran into his house to telephone for help. He was terrified.

Within a few minutes a red, shiny fire engine came racing along the road. It stopped outside Mr Munemo's gate. The firemen jumped down and began to roll out a long hose.

'Connect the hose over there,' shouted the leader, pointing at the hydrant across the road. Two firemen ran across with one end of the long hose and quickly clipped it on.

'Ready?' asked the leader.

Everyone waited to see what would happen next.

By now there were lots of people standing outside Mr Munemo's house. The smoke from the fire was thick and grey. They covered their mouths and watched the firemen point their hose at the fire.

Mr Munemo was jumping up and down and waving his arms wildly. He was careful not to get too close to the fire.

'Do something!' he screamed. 'Hurry up or it will be too late. I'll lose my house.'

'Turn it on!' shouted the leader.

The people held their breath. They stared at the open end of the thick hose and waited – and waited. The two firemen who held the end tightly looked down, surprised.

Nothing was happening!

Then, a slow trickle of water dripped out of the hose on to the ground. It lasted for only a few seconds and then it stopped. The hot sun soon began to dry up the drops that had spilled.

Mr Munemo screamed even louder. 'What's the matter? Put this fire out now, before my house burns down.' He was so angry that he was dancing with rage.

'I can't understand it,' said the leading fireman. He called again across the road, 'Turn it on!'

Still nothing happened. There was not even a drop of water this time. The firemen were puzzled. The people all shook their heads.

Then a voice said, 'It's Tuesday.'

Everyone looked round, and then down. A small girl had spoken. 'It's Tuesday,' she said again.

The people stared at each other and then at the girl. 'What do you mean?' asked one.

The little girl explained, 'There's no water in Mutare on a Tuesday, or a Thursday or Saturday. It's switched off.'

'Of course!' said the people, nodding. Everyone had forgotten that Mutare was dry for three days a week. This was still a new law in the town. 'No one has water on a Tuesday, not even the Fire Brigade.'

'Not even Mr Munemo,' laughed one man.

Mr Munemo rushed up to the leading fireman. He was so angry that he stamped his foot.

'What are you going to do?' he demanded.

'Perhaps the wind will change,' said the fireman.

'Wait a minute,' said Mr Munemo's nearest neighbour.

'What is it?' asked the fireman.

'That water tank is full. It was filled with water this morning. I saw the truck here and heard the pump working.'

'No!' cried Mr Munemo. 'That water was very expensive. It cost a fortune.'

'I don't care,' said the fireman. 'Our job is to put out the fire.' He turned and shouted, 'There's water in the tank.'

The firemen moved very quickly. They dragged the hose across the road and ran to the water tank. They attached the end of the hose to the outlet pipe at the bottom of the tank.

'Right,' said the leading fireman. 'Turn the tap on!'

Soon water was pouring out of the hose. It poured on to the flames near the house first. Then it poured on to the burning lawn. Lastly, the hose was turned on to the hedge.

Clouds of steam rose into the air when the cool water splashed on to the flames. The noise was like a snake hissing.

'There's not much water left,' called the man on top of the platform.

The leader replied, 'Don't worry. We've nearly finished.'

And then the last flame died. The fire was out and Mr Munemo's house was safe. The people cheered. The firemen smiled and waved. Everyone was happy – except Mr Munemo.

The firemen said to him, 'We'll have to charge you for putting out the fire.'

The welder said, 'I'll be back to finish the job and then I'll send in your bill.'

As everybody left, Mr Munemo stood looking sadly all around him.

'My garden is ruined and the gate is still broken,' he moaned. 'I've lost lots of money. And I'm left with an empty water tank.'

He turned and walked slowly up his driveway. It had been a bad day for him.

Questions

1 What happens in times of drought on the farms?
2 How do people in towns try to save water when there is a drought?
3 Why did Mr Munemo want to have more water?
4 What did he do to get more water?
5 How do you think his neighbours felt about his water tank?
6 How did the fire in Mr Munemo's garden get started?
7 Why could the firemen not get their hose to work?
8 How did the firemen solve the problem?
9 Why was Mr Munemo unhappy with the firemen, even though they saved his house?

Activities

1 Find out from people in your area what they remember about times of drought. Tell the class what you find out.
2 Think about ways in which you could save water. Draw pictures to make people in your school think about saving water.
3 If there had been no water in the tank, how do you think the story would have ended?

Glossary

bill (page 27) a note that tells you how much to pay for something

borehole (page 5) an underground water supply

drought (page 1) a time of great dryness, when the rain does not fall for a long time

fierce (page 14) strong, intense

Fire Brigade (page 17) a team of people whose job is to put out fires

hydrant (page 18) a pipe that leads to a main water pipe underground

puzzled (page 21) unable to understand why something is happening

rage (page 10) terrible anger

trickle (page 20) a very thin stream

welder (page 12) a person who uses flame to soften and repair metal

The Junior African Writers Series is designed to provide interesting and varied African stories both for pleasure and for study. There are five graded levels in the series.

Level 2 is suited to readers who have been studying English for four to five years. The content and language have been carefully controlled to increase fluency in reading.

Content The plots are simple and the number of characters is kept to a minimum. The information is presented in small manageable amounts and the illustrations reinforce the text.

Language Reading is a learning experience and, although the choice of new words is carefully controlled, new words that are important to the story are also introduced. These are contextualised and explained in the glossary. They also appear in other stories at Level 2.

Glossary Difficult words which learners may not know have been listed alphabetically at the back of the book. The definitions refer to the way a word is used in the story, and the page reference is for the word's first use.

Questions and **Activities** The questions give useful comprehension practice and ensure that the reader has followed and understood the story. The activities develop themes and ideas introduced and can be done as pairwork or groupwork in class, or as homework.

JAWS Starters
In addition to the five levels of JAWS titles, there are three levels of JAWS Starters. These are full-colour picture books designed to lead in to the first level of JAWS.